Sabrina Carpenter

Biography For Kids

Singing, Acting, and Never Giving Up

Benjamin Danielson

This book belongs to……………………

……………………………………………

COPYRIGHT © 2024 by Benjamin Danielson

All rights reserved. No part of this publication may be reproduced, distributed, or transmitted in any form or by any means, including photocopying, recording, or other electronic or mechanical methods, without the prior written permission of the publisher, except in the case of brief quotations embodied in critical reviews and certain other noncommercial uses permitted by copyright law.

Trademarks and pictures are used without permission. Use of the trademark is not authorized by, associated with, or sponsored by the trademark owners. All trademarks and pictures used within this book are used with no intent to infringe on the trademark owners and only used for clarifying purposes.

TABLE OF CONTENTS

INTRODUCTION

WHO IS SABRINA CARPENTER?

SABRINA'S MUSIC JOURNEY

SABRINA'S ACTING CAREER

SABRINA'S STYLE AND FASHION

SABRINA'S LIFE LESSONS

FUN FACTS ABOUT SABRINA

SABRINA'S IMPACT ON THE WORLD

A TIMELINE OF LIFE AND CAREER

GLOSSARY OF TERMS EXPLAINED

SABRINA CARPENTER QUIZ

INTRODUCTION

<u>A Brief Overview Of Sabrina Carpenter</u>

Sabrina Carpenter is a talented singer, actress, and songwriter. She is best known for her role as Riley Matthews in the Disney Channel show "Girl Meets World." Sabrina has also released several successful albums, including "Eyes Wide Open," "Evolution," and "Singular."

Why should you read this book?

This book is a must-read for anyone who wants to be inspired. Sabrina Carpenter's story is one of hard work, dedication, and perseverance. She has achieved great success, and she is an inspiration to young people around the world.

What will you learn from this book?

You will learn about Sabrina Carpenter's life and career. You will also learn about her inspiring message of following your dreams and never giving up.

CHAPTER 1:

WHO IS SABRINA CARPENTER?

Sabrina Carpenter is a shining star who has captured the hearts of millions around the world with her incredible talent and infectious personality. She's not just a singer and actress; she's a role model, a friend, and an inspiration to countless young people.

Sabrina was born on May 11, 1999, in Philadelphia, Pennsylvania. Growing up, she was surrounded by a loving family who supported her dreams from the very beginning. Her parents, Elizabeth and David Carpenter, always encouraged her to pursue her passions, whether it was singing, dancing, or acting.

As a little girl, Sabrina was always putting on shows for her family and friends. She loved to dress up in costumes, sing along to her favorite songs, and pretend to be a famous actress. Her parents saw her natural talent and knew that she had a special gift.

When Sabrina was 11 years old, she auditioned for a local theater production of "Annie." She landed the lead role and quickly realized that she had found her calling. After the show, a talent agent approached Sabrina and offered to represent her. It was the beginning of her journey to stardom.

Sabrina's big break came when she was cast in the Disney Channel show "Girl Meets World." The show was a huge success, and Sabrina became a household name overnight. She played the role of Riley Matthews, a bright and curious teenager who navigates the ups and downs of high school.

In addition to her acting career, Sabrina also began to pursue her passion for music. She released her debut album, "Eyes Wide Open," in 2015, and it quickly became a hit. Sabrina's songs are catchy, relatable, and often deal with themes of love, heartbreak, and self-discovery.

One of Sabrina's most popular songs is "Why," which she co-wrote with Jonas Brothers' Nick Jonas. The song is a powerful anthem about overcoming challenges and never giving up on your dreams. Sabrina's lyrics are heartfelt and inspiring, and the song has resonated with fans of all ages.

Sabrina is not only a talented singer and actress, but she is also a kind and generous person. She is passionate about using her platform to make a positive impact on the world. Sabrina has supported various charities, including the Make-A-Wish Foundation and the Trevor Project. She believes that everyone has the power to make a difference, no matter how small.

"I think it's important to use your voice and your platform to stand up for what you believe in,"

Sabrina has said. "I want to inspire people to be themselves and to follow their dreams."

Sabrina's journey to stardom has been filled with ups and downs, but she has always persevered. She has faced challenges, but she has never given up on her dreams. Sabrina's story is a testament to the power of hard work, dedication, and believing in yourself.

"I've learned that it's okay to make mistakes," Sabrina has said. "It's how you learn and grow. The most important thing is to never give up on yourself."

Family and Friends

Sabrina's family has been a constant source of love and support throughout her life. She often speaks about how grateful she is for her parents, Elizabeth and David, and her siblings, Eric and Shannon.

Her parents have always been her biggest cheerleaders. They have supported her dreams, attended all of her performances, and been there for her through thick and thin. Sabrina's mom, Elizabeth, is a talented artist, and her dad, David, is a successful businessman. They have instilled in Sabrina a strong work ethic and a passion for creativity.

Sabrina's siblings, Eric and Shannon, are also a huge part of her life. They are her best friends and confidants. The three of them often spend time together, hanging out, playing games, and simply enjoying each other's company.

Sabrina's family has had a significant impact on her career. Her parents have helped her navigate the entertainment industry, and her siblings have always been there to offer advice and encouragement.

In addition to her family, Sabrina has a close circle of friends who she considers to be like family. She has known some of her friends since childhood, and they have been there for her through all of life's ups and downs.

One of Sabrina's closest friends is the singer and actress Olivia Rodrigo.

The two met while working together on the Disney Channel show "Bunk'd." They quickly became best friends and have supported each other's careers.

"Olivia is like a sister to me," Sabrina has said. **"We've been through a lot together, and we're always there for each other."**

Sabrina's friends are a source of inspiration and support for her. They encourage her to be herself, to follow her dreams, and to never give up.

"My friends are my biggest cheerleaders," Sabrina has said. **"They believe in me more than I sometimes believe in myself."**

Sabrina's family and friends have played a crucial role in her success. They have provided her with love, support, and encouragement, and they have helped her to become the amazing person she is today.

"**I am so grateful for my family and friends,**" Sabrina has said. "**They are my everything.**"

Early Days of Acting and Singing

From a young age, Sabrina was always drawn to the stage. She loved to perform, whether it was singing along to her favorite songs or putting on plays for her family and friends. Her parents recognized her talent and encouraged her to pursue her passion.

When Sabrina auditioned for a local theater when she was just 11 years old, she produced "Annie." She landed the lead role and quickly realized that she had found her calling. The experience was a turning point in her life, and it gave her the confidence to pursue a career in the arts.

After the "Annie" production, Sabrina began to take acting lessons and participate in local theater productions. She also started taking singing lessons and joined a choir. She was determined to hone her skills and become the best performer she could be.

In addition to her acting and singing pursuits, Sabrina was also involved in other activities, such as dancing and playing sports. She was a well-rounded student and always had a lot of energy.

As Sabrina grew older, she began to dream of becoming a professional actress and singer. She knew that it would be a challenging path, but she was determined to make it happen.

"I always knew that I wanted to be on stage," Sabrina has said. **"It's where I feel most comfortable and most at home."**

Sabrina's early days of acting and singing were filled with excitement, passion, and hard work. She was determined to make her dreams a reality, and she was willing to do whatever it took to succeed.

CHAPTER 2:

SABRINA'S MUSIC JOURNEY

First Albums and Songs

Sabrina's music journey began in earnest when she was a teenager. She started writing songs and performing at local venues. Her early songs were a mix of pop, rock, and country influences, and they reflected her personal experiences and emotions.

In 2014, Sabrina released her debut EP, "Can't Blame a Girl for Trying." The EP was a collection of catchy pop songs that showcased her vocal abilities and songwriting talent. The EP was well-received by critics and fans alike, and it helped to establish Sabrina as a rising star in the music industry.

The following year, Sabrina released her debut album, "Eyes Wide Open." The album was a mix of upbeat pop songs and more introspective ballads. The album's singles, "Why" and "Smoke and Fire," were both huge hits, and they helped to propel Sabrina to stardom.

Sabrina's music is known for its catchy melodies, relatable lyrics, and powerful vocals. She often writes about personal experiences, such as love, heartbreak, and self-discovery. Her songs are both uplifting and empowering, and they resonate with fans of all ages.

Sabrina's music has evolved over the years, but she has always remained true to herself. She is not afraid to experiment with different genres and styles, and she is always pushing herself to grow as an artist.

In addition to her own music, Sabrina has also collaborated with other artists, including Nick Jonas, Shawn Mendes, and Bastille. These collaborations have helped to expand her fanbase and introduce her to new audiences.

"I love collaborating with other artists," Sabrina has said. **"It's a great way to learn and grow as an artist."**

Sabrina's music journey has been filled with ups and downs, but she has always persevered. She has faced challenges, but she has never given up on her dreams. Sabrina's music is a testament to the power of hard work, dedication, and believing in yourself.

"I'm so grateful for the opportunity to make music," Sabrina has said. **"It's my passion, and it's what I love to do."**

Breakthrough Hits

Sabrina's music career took off in 2015 with the release of her debut album, **"Eyes Wide Open."** The album's singles, "Why" and "Smoke and Fire," were both huge hits, and they helped to propel Sabrina to stardom.

"Why" was a powerful anthem about overcoming challenges and never giving up on your dreams. The song resonated with fans of all ages, and it became a viral hit on social media.

"**Smoke and Fire**" was a catchy pop song about young love and heartbreak. The song's music video was also a hit, and it featured Sabrina dancing and having fun with her friends.

The success of "Why" and "Smoke and Fire" helped to establish Sabrina as a rising star in the music industry. She began to tour the world, and her concerts were selling out.

In 2017, Sabrina released her second studio album, "Singular." The album was a departure from her previous work, and it featured a more mature sound. The album's singles, "Thumbs Up" and "Alien," were both successful, and they further cemented Sabrina's status as a pop star.

Sabrina's music has continued to evolve over the years. She has released several more albums and singles, and she has collaborated with other artists, such as Nick Jonas, Shawn Mendes, and Bastille.

Some of Sabrina's other popular songs include:

1. "Hallelujah"
2. "Skin"
3. "The Way I Love You"

4. "Good at Guys"

5. "We're Not Strangers"

Sabrina's music is known for its catchy melodies, relatable lyrics, and powerful vocals. She often writes about personal experiences, such as love, heartbreak, and self-discovery. Her songs are both uplifting and empowering, and they resonate with fans of all ages.

"I want my music to make people feel good," Sabrina has said. "I want to create songs that people can connect with and that will stay with them for a long time."

Sabrina's breakthrough hits have helped to make her one of the most popular pop stars of her generation. She has a dedicated fanbase, and her music continues to inspire and entertain people around the world.

Touring and Live Performances

Sabrina's music has taken her all over the world. She has toured extensively, playing concerts in sold-out arenas and stadiums. Her live performances are known for their energy, passion, and connection with the audience.

Sabrina loves to interact with her fans during her concerts. She often talks to the crowd, takes selfies, and even jumps into the audience to greet her fans. Her concerts are always a memorable experience for everyone involved.

"I love performing live," Sabrina has said. **"It's the best feeling in the world to be on stage and sharing my music with my fans."**

Sabrina's tours are often accompanied by merchandise, such

as t-shirts, posters, and albums. She also sells exclusive items at her shows, such as limited edition vinyl records and signed memorabilia.

In addition to her headlining tours, Sabrina has also performed at festivals and other events around the world. She has shared the stage with some of the biggest names in music, including Taylor Swift, Shawn Mendes, and Ed Sheeran.

"**It's been amazing to perform with so many talented artists,**" Sabrina has said. "**I've learned a lot from them, and I'm grateful for the opportunities I've had.**"

Sabrina's live performances are always a highlight of her music career. She loves to connect with her fans and share her passion for music with the world.

"I'm so grateful for the support of my fans," Sabrina has said. **"They are the reason I do what I do."**

Sabrina's touring and live performances have helped to cement her status as one of the most popular pop stars of her generation. Her concerts are always a memorable experience, and they continue to inspire and entertain people around the world.

CHAPTER 3:

SABRINA'S ACTING CAREER

Disney Channel Star

Sabrina's acting career took off in 2012 when she was cast in the Disney Channel show "Girl Meets World." The show was a sequel to the popular 90s sitcom "Boy Meets World," and it followed the adventures of Riley

Matthews, a bright and curious teenager.

Sabrina played the role of Riley Matthews, a character who was much like herself in many ways. Riley was a kind and caring girl who loved to learn and explore. She was also a bit of a dreamer, and she often found herself in funny and embarrassing situations.

"Girl Meets World" was a huge success, and Sabrina became a household name. She appeared in all three seasons of the show, and she starred in several Disney Channel movies, including "Adventures in Babysitting" and "Stuck in the Middle."

Sabrina's time on the Disney Channel was a formative experience for her. She learned a lot about acting, and she made many lifelong friends. She also gained a huge following of young fans who looked up to her as a role model.

"I'm so grateful for my time on the Disney Channel," Sabrina has said. **"It was a dream come true."**

Sabrina's experience on the Disney Channel helped to prepare her for her future career. She learned how to handle the pressures of fame, and she developed a strong work ethic.

She also learned the importance of being a positive role model for young people.

"I want to be a role model for kids," Sabrina has said. "I **want to show them that anything is possible if you work hard and believe in yourself.**"

Sabrina's time on the Disney Channel was a major milestone in her career. It helped to launch her to stardom, and it gave her the confidence to pursue her dreams.

Movies and TV Shows

After her time on the Disney Channel, Sabrina continued to pursue her acting career. She appeared in several movies and TV shows, **including**:

1. **The Hate U Give** (2018)
2. **Looking Glass** (2019)

3. **The Short History of the Long Road** (2021)

4. **Emergency** (2022)

5. **The Summoning** (2023)

Sabrina's roles in these movies and TV shows were diverse and challenging. She played a variety of characters, from a rebellious teenager to a haunted woman. Her performances were praised by critics, and she was nominated for several awards.

One of Sabrina's most notable roles was in the film "The Hate U Give." The film was based on a critically acclaimed novel by Angie Thomas, and it explored themes of racism, police brutality, and social justice. Sabrina played the role of Starr Carter, a 16-year-old girl who witnesses the police shooting of her unarmed best friend.

Sabrina's performance in "The Hate U Give" was praised for its honesty and authenticity. She brought the character of Starr to life in a powerful and moving way. The film was a critical and commercial success, and it helped to raise awareness of important social issues.

"I'm so proud of 'The Hate U Give,'" Sabrina has said. **"It's a film that has had a real impact on people's lives."**

Sabrina's acting career has continued to flourish in recent years.

She has taken on challenging roles, and she has proven herself to be a versatile and talented actress. She is a rising star in Hollywood, and she is sure to have many more successes in the years to come.

"I love acting," Sabrina has said. **"It's my passion, and it's what I love to do."**

Sabrina's acting career has been a major part of her life. She has starred in many successful movies and TV shows, and she has proven herself to be a talented and versatile actress. She is a rising star in Hollywood, and she is sure to have many more successes in the years to come.

Voice Acting

In addition to her live-action roles, Sabrina has also done a lot of voice acting work. She has voiced characters in animated movies, TV shows, and video games.

One of Sabrina's most notable voice acting roles was in the animated movie "Ralph Breaks the Internet." She voiced the character of Ramona, a popular video game character who becomes friends with Ralph.

Sabrina's performance in "Ralph Breaks the Internet" was praised for its energy and enthusiasm. She brought the character of Ramona to life in a fun and engaging way. The movie was a huge success, and it helped to further establish Sabrina as a talented voice actress.

Sabrina has also voiced characters in several animated TV shows, including "Tangled: The Series" and "Milo Murphy's Law." She has also voiced characters in video games, such as "Kingdom Hearts III" and "Lego DC Super-Villains."

Voice acting is a challenging form of acting, but Sabrina has proven herself to be a natural at it. She is able to bring a wide range of characters to life, and she is able to convey a variety of emotions through her voice.

"I love voice acting," Sabrina has said. "It's a really fun and creative process."

Sabrina's voice acting work has helped to expand her career and introduce her to new audiences. She is a talented and versatile actress, and she is sure to have many more successes in the years to come.

"I'm so grateful for all of the opportunities I've had," Sabrina has said. **"I'm just getting started."**

Sabrina's voice acting work has been a major part of her career. She has voiced characters in many successful animated movies, TV shows, and video games. She is a talented and versatile actress, and she is sure to have many more successes in the years to come.

CHAPTER 4:

SABRINA'S STYLE AND FASHION

Red Carpet Looks

Sabrina is known for her stylish and sophisticated sense of fashion. She often makes headlines for her stunning red carpet looks.

Sabrina's red carpet style is typically glamorous and feminine. She loves to wear dresses in bold colors and eye-catching designs. She also enjoys experimenting with different trends and styles.

One of Sabrina's signature looks is a flowing gown with a plunging neckline. She often pairs these dresses with statement jewelry and bold makeup.

Sabrina is not afraid to take risks with her fashion choices. She has been seen in everything from vintage-inspired looks to futuristic outfits. She is always looking for ways to stand out and make a statement.

"I love to experiment with fashion," Sabrina has said. "I'm not afraid to try new things."

Sabrina's red carpet looks are always a highlight of any event. She is a fashion icon, and her style is admired by fans and fashion critics alike.

"Sabrina has a natural sense of style," one fashion critic said. **"She always looks amazing on the red carpet."**

Sabrina's red carpet looks are a reflection of her personality. She is confident, stylish, and unafraid to be herself. She is a role model for young people, and her fashion sense is an inspiration to many.

"I want to inspire people to be themselves and to express themselves through their fashion," Sabrina has said.

Sabrina's red carpet looks are a testament to her style and sophistication. She is a fashion icon, and her style is admired by fans and fashion critics alike.

Everyday Style

While Sabrina's red carpet looks are always stunning, her everyday style is just as impressive. She has a casual and effortless style that is both comfortable and chic.

Sabrina often wears jeans and a t-shirt or a casual dress. She loves to accessorize her outfits with hats, scarves, and jewelry. She also has a collection of stylish sneakers and boots.

Sabrina is not afraid to mix and match different styles. She often combines high-end designer pieces with affordable finds. She is always on the lookout for new trends, and she is not afraid to experiment with her wardrobe.

"I love to shop," Sabrina has said. **"I'm always looking for new pieces to add to my wardrobe."**

Sabrina's everyday style is both relatable and inspiring. She shows that it is possible to look stylish without breaking the bank. She is also a role model for young people, and her fashion sense is an inspiration to many.

"I want to show people that you can be stylish on a budget," Sabrina has said.

Sabrina's everyday style is a reflection of her personality. She is comfortable, confident, and unafraid to be herself. She is a fashion icon, and her style is admired by fans and fashion critics alike.

Sabrina's everyday style is a testament to her versatility. She can dress up or down depending on the occasion, and she always looks amazing. She is a fashion icon, and her style is an inspiration to many.

"I hope my style inspires people to be themselves and to express themselves through their fashion," Sabrina has said.

Sabrina's everyday style is a reflection of her personality. She is comfortable, confident, and unafraid to be herself. She is a fashion icon, and her style is admired by fans and fashion critics alike.

Favorite Brands

Sabrina is a fan of many different fashion brands. She is often seen wearing clothes and accessories from popular designers, such as:

1. **Gucci**
2. **Louis Vuitton**

3. **Chanel**

4. **Dior**

5. **Nike**

6. **Adidas**

Sabrina loves the classic and timeless designs of Gucci and Louis Vuitton. She also appreciates the luxury and craftsmanship of Chanel and Dior. She is a fan of athletic wear, and she often wears clothes and shoes from Nike and Adidas.

Sabrina is not afraid to mix and match different brands. She often pairs high-end designer pieces with affordable finds. She is always on the lookout for new trends, and she is not afraid to experiment with her wardrobe.

Sabrina's favorite brands are a reflection of her personality. She is stylish, sophisticated, and unafraid to be herself. She is a fashion icon, and her style is admired by fans and fashion critics alike.

"Sabrina has a great sense of style," one fashion critic said. "**She always looks put together, even when she's just running errands.**"

Sabrina's favorite brands are a testament to her versatility. She can dress up or down depending on the occasion, and she always looks amazing. She is a fashion icon, and her style is an inspiration to many.

Sabrina's favorite brands are a reflection of her personality. She is stylish, sophisticated, and unafraid to be herself. She is a fashion icon, and her style is admired by fans and fashion critics alike.

CHAPTER 5:

SABRINA'S LIFE LESSONS

Overcoming Challenges

Sabrina has faced many challenges in her life, but she has always persevered. She has learned important lessons along the way, and she has become a stronger person as a result.

One of the biggest challenges Sabrina has faced is the pressure of fame. As a young celebrity, she has had to deal with the constant attention of the media and the public. She has also had to learn how to navigate the ups and downs of the entertainment industry.

"It's not always easy being in the spotlight," Sabrina has said. "But I've learned to focus on the positive and to ignore the negativity."

Sabrina has also faced challenges with her body image. She has been open about her struggles with body dysmorphia, and she has used her platform to raise awareness about this issue.

"It's important to love yourself for who you are," Sabrina has said. **"Don't let anyone tell you that you're not good enough."**

Sabrina has also faced challenges in her personal life. She has experienced heartbreak and loss, but she has always found a way to move forward.

"Life is full of ups and downs," Sabrina has said. **"But it's important to keep your head up and keep going."**

Sabrina has learned a lot about herself through her challenges. She has become a stronger, more resilient person. She has also learned the importance of perseverance, resilience, and self-love.

"I'm proud of who I am today," Sabrina has said. **"I've overcome a lot of challenges, and I'm stronger because of it."**

Sabrina's life lessons are an inspiration to many. She has shown that it is possible to overcome challenges and to live a fulfilling life. Her story is a testament to the power of perseverance, resilience, and self-love.

"No matter what you're going through, never give up on yourself," Sabrina has said. "You are stronger than you think."

Being Yourself

Another important lesson Sabrina has learned is the importance of being yourself. She has always been true to herself, and she has never let anyone tell her who to be.

"It's important to be authentic," Sabrina has said. "Don't try to be someone you're not."

Sabrina has always been confident in her own skin. She is not afraid to express herself and to be different. She believes that everyone is unique, and that we should all embrace our individuality.

"Everyone is special in their own way," Sabrina has said. **"Don't be afraid to be yourself."**

Sabrina has also learned the importance of not caring what other people think. She has always been true to herself, even when it has been difficult. She believes that it is better to be true to yourself than to try to please everyone else.

"Don't let anyone bring you down," Sabrina has said. "**You are amazing just the way you are.**"

Sabrina's message of being yourself is an important one for young people. She has shown that it is possible to be successful and happy without conforming to society's expectations.

"I'm proud to be who I am," Sabrina has said. **"I'm not afraid to be different."**

Sabrina's life lessons are an inspiration to many. She has shown that it is possible to overcome challenges and to live a fulfilling life. Her story is a testament to the power of perseverance, resilience, self-love, and being yourself.

"Be yourself, and don't let anyone tell you who to be," Sabrina has said. **"You are amazing just the way you are."**

Following Your Dreams

Another important lesson Sabrina has learned is the importance of following your dreams. She has always been passionate about her career, and she has never given up on her goals.

"**If you have a dream, go for it,**" Sabrina has said. "**Don't let anyone tell you that you can't do it.**"

Sabrina has faced many challenges along the way, but she has never given up on her dreams. She has worked hard, and she has persevered. Her hard work and dedication have paid off, and she has achieved great success.

"**It takes a lot of hard work to achieve your dreams,**" Sabrina has said. "**But it's all worth it in the end.**"

Sabrina's message of following your dreams is an important one for young people. She has shown that it is possible to achieve your goals, no matter how difficult it may seem.

"Don't let anyone tell you that you can't do it," Sabrina has said. "Believe in yourself and keep going."

Sabrina's life lessons are an inspiration to many. She has shown that it is possible to overcome challenges and to live a fulfilling life. Her story is a testament to the power of perseverance, resilience, self-love, being yourself, and following your dreams.

"Be yourself, and don't let anyone tell you who to be," Sabrina has said. "You are amazing just the way you are."

Sabrina's life lessons are an inspiration to young people around the world. She has shown that it is possible to achieve your dreams, no matter how difficult it may seem.

CHAPTER 6:

FUN FACTS ABOUT SABRINA

Hobbies and Interests

Sabrina is a talented and versatile person. She has many hobbies and interests outside of her career. Here are some fun facts about Sabrina:

1. **She loves to read.** Sabrina is a bookworm, and she loves to lose

herself in a good story. Her favorite genres are fantasy and young adult fiction.

2. **She is a talented artist.** Sabrina enjoys painting and drawing. She has even created her own line of merchandise, including t-shirts and phone cases.

3. **She is a dog lover.** Sabrina has a pet dog named Charlie, who she loves dearly. She often shares

photos of Charlie on social media.

4. **She is a sports fan.** Sabrina is a fan of basketball and soccer. She enjoys watching games and cheering for her favorite teams.

5. **She is a foodie.** Sabrina loves to try new foods, and she is a great cook. She often shares her favorite recipes on social media.

6. **She is a nature lover.** Sabrina enjoys spending time outdoors.

She loves to go hiking, camping, and swimming.

7. **She is a philanthropist.** Sabrina is passionate about giving back to the community. She has supported many charities, including the Make-A-Wish Foundation and the Trevor Project.

These are just a few of Sabrina's many hobbies and interests. She is a talented and versatile person, and she is always finding new things to do.

"I love to keep myself busy," Sabrina has said. **"I'm always looking for new things to learn and explore."**

Sabrina's hobbies and interests are a reflection of her personality. She is a creative, adventurous, and compassionate person. She is a role model for young people, and her hobbies and interests are an inspiration to many.

"I hope my hobbies and interests inspire people to try new things and to follow their passions," Sabrina has said.

Sabrina's hobbies and interests are a testament to her versatility. She is a talented and creative person, and she is always finding new things to do. She is a role model for young people, and her hobbies and interests are an inspiration to many.

"I'm so grateful for all of the opportunities I've had," Sabrina has said. **"I'm just getting started."**

Sabrina's hobbies and interests are a reflection of her personality. She is a creative, adventurous, and compassionate person. She is a role model for young people, and her hobbies and interests are an inspiration to many.

Favorite Foods and Music

Sabrina has a variety of favorite foods. She loves to try new things, but she also has some go-to dishes that she always enjoys. Here are a few of Sabrina's favorite foods:

1. **Pizza:** Sabrina is a big fan of pizza, especially pepperoni and mushroom.

2. **Pasta:** Sabrina loves pasta, especially spaghetti and meatballs.

3. **Sushi:** Sabrina is a sushi lover. She enjoys trying different types of sushi, and she is a fan of spicy tuna rolls.

4. **Tacos:** Sabrina is a big fan of Mexican food, and she loves

tacos. She is a fan of both street tacos and restaurant tacos.

5. **Ice cream:** Sabrina has a sweet tooth, and she loves ice cream. Her favorite flavors are chocolate, vanilla, and cookie dough.

Sabrina also has a variety of favorite music artists. She loves listening to a wide range of genres, from pop and rock to country and hip-hop. Here are a few of Sabrina's favorite artists:

1. **Taylor Swift:** Sabrina is a big fan of Taylor Swift. She loves her catchy pop songs and her heartfelt lyrics.

2. **Ed Sheeran:** Sabrina is also a fan of Ed Sheeran. She loves his acoustic songs and his soulful voice.

3. **Ariana Grande:** Sabrina is a fan of Ariana Grande. She loves her

powerful vocals and her catchy pop songs.

4. **The Weeknd:** Sabrina is a fan of The Weeknd. She loves his dark and moody music.

5. **Beyoncé:** Sabrina is a fan of Beyoncé. She loves her powerful vocals and her inspiring lyrics.

Sabrina's favorite foods and music are a reflection of her personality. She is a fun-loving and adventurous person who enjoys trying new things. She is also a passionate music fan, and she loves to discover new artists.

"I love to explore new music," Sabrina has said. "I'm always looking for new artists to discover."

Sabrina's favorite foods and music are a testament to her versatility. She is a person of many interests, and she is always finding new things to enjoy.

Sabrina's favorite foods and music are a reflection of her personality. She is a fun-loving and adventurous person who enjoys trying new things. She is also a passionate music fan, and she loves to discover new artists.

Behind-the-Scenes Stories

Sabrina has shared many behind-the-scenes stories about her life and career. Here are a few of her most interesting stories:

1. **The time she met Taylor Swift:** Sabrina was a big fan of Taylor Swift growing up. She met Taylor Swift at a concert and

was so excited that she couldn't speak.

2. **The time she got lost in Paris:** Sabrina once got lost in Paris while filming a music video. She was able to find her way back to her hotel with the help of a friendly stranger.

3. **The time she was a guest on Jimmy Fallon:** Sabrina appeared on The Tonight Show with Jimmy Fallon. She played a

game of "Wheel of Fortune" and had a lot of fun.

4. **The time she met her celebrity crush:** Sabrina has met many of her celebrity crushes over the years. She has met people like Ryan Reynolds, Chris Hemsworth, and Harry Styles.

5. **The time she got a tattoo:** Sabrina has a few tattoos. She got her first tattoo when she was 18 years old.

6. **The time she went on a road trip:** Sabrina once went on a road trip with her friends. They drove across the country and had a lot of fun.

7. **The time she got a haircut:** Sabrina has changed her hairstyle many times over the years. She once got a pixie cut and she loved it.

These are just a few of Sabrina's many behind-the-scenes stories.

She is a fun-loving and adventurous person, and she always has interesting stories to tell.

"**I've had so many amazing experiences,**" Sabrina has said. "**I'm so grateful for everything I've been through.**"

Sabrina's behind-the-scenes stories are a testament to her versatility. She is a talented and creative person, and she is always finding new things to do. She is a role model for young people, and her stories are an inspiration to many.

"I hope my stories inspire people to follow their dreams and to have fun," Sabrina has said.

Sabrina's behind-the-scenes stories are a reflection of her personality. She is a fun-loving and adventurous person who loves to share her experiences. She is a role model for young people, and her stories are an inspiration to many.

"I'm so grateful for all of the opportunities I've had," Sabrina has said. **"I'm just getting started."**

Sabrina's behind-the-scenes stories are a testament to her versatility. She is a talented and creative person, and she is always finding new things to do. She is a role model for young people, and her stories are an inspiration to many.

CHAPTER 7:

SABRINA'S IMPACT ON THE WORLD

Role Model for Kids

Sabrina is a role model for millions of young people around the world. She is a positive force in the entertainment industry, and she uses her platform to inspire others.

Sabrina is a great role model for kids because she is kind, caring, and hardworking. She is always willing to help others, and she is a great example of what it means to be a good person.

Sabrina is also a great role model for kids because she is talented and successful. She has achieved great things in her career, and she is an inspiration to many young people who dream of following in her footsteps.

"I want to be a role model for kids," Sabrina has said. **"I want to show them that anything is possible if you work hard and believe in yourself."**

Sabrina is a great role model for kids because she is always true to herself. She is not afraid to be different, and she is an inspiration to young people who are struggling to find their own identity.

"**Be yourself, and don't let anyone tell you who to be,**" Sabrina has said. "**You are amazing just the way you are.**"

Sabrina is a great role model for kids because she is a positive force in the world. She uses her platform to raise awareness about important social issues, and she is an inspiration to young people who want to make a difference.

"**I want to use my voice to make a positive impact on the world,**" Sabrina has said. "**I want to inspire people to be kind, caring, and compassionate.**"

Sabrina is a great role model for kids in many ways. She is kind, caring, hardworking, talented, successful, and true to herself. She is an inspiration to young people who want to make a difference in the world.

"I'm so grateful for the opportunity to be a role model for kids," Sabrina has said. **"It's the greatest honor of my life."**

Sabrina is a role model for millions of young people around the world. She is a positive force in the entertainment industry, and she uses her platform to inspire others. She is a great example of what it means to be a kind, caring, hardworking, talented, successful, and true to yourself. She is an inspiration to young people who want to make a difference in the world.

Charity Work and Giving Back

Sabrina is a passionate philanthropist. She is committed to giving back to the community, and she supports many charities.

One of the charities that Sabrina is most passionate about is the Make-A-Wish Foundation. This charity grants wishes to children with life-threatening illnesses.

Sabrina has met many Make-A-Wish children, and she has been inspired by their courage and resilience.

"It's an honor to be able to grant wishes to these amazing kids," Sabrina has said. "They are true heroes."

Sabrina is also a supporter of the Trevor Project, a crisis intervention and suicide prevention service for LGBTQ+ youth. Sabrina believes that everyone should feel safe and accepted, regardless of their sexual orientation or gender identity.

"It's important to create a safe and inclusive environment for everyone," Sabrina has said. **"Everyone deserves to feel loved and accepted."**

Sabrina is also a supporter of the World Wildlife Fund. This organization works to protect endangered species and their habitats. Sabrina is a passionate animal lover, and she is committed to protecting the planet for future generations.

"We need to take care of our planet," Sabrina has said. **"It's the only one we have."**

Sabrina is a role model for young people who want to make a difference in the world. She is passionate about giving back, and she is an inspiration to others.

"**I believe that everyone has the power** to make a difference," Sabrina has said. "**No matter how small,** every act of kindness **counts.**"

Sabrina's charity work is a testament to her compassion and generosity. She is a role model for young people who want to make a difference in the world.

"I'm so grateful for the opportunity to give back," Sabrina has said. **"It's the most rewarding thing I've ever done."**

Sabrina's charity work is a testament to her compassion and generosity. She is a role model for young people who want to make a difference in the world. She is an inspiration to others, and she is making a positive impact on the world.

Inspiring Others

Sabrina is an inspiration to millions of young people around the world. She is a positive force in the entertainment industry, and she uses her platform to inspire others to be their best selves.

Sabrina is an inspiration to young people because she is kind, caring, and hardworking. She is always willing to help others, and she is a great example of what it means to be a good person.

Sabrina is also an inspiration to young people because she is talented and successful. She has achieved great things in her career, and she is an inspiration to many young people who dream of following in her footsteps.

"I want to inspire people to be their best selves," Sabrina has said. **"I want to show them that anything is possible if you work hard and believe in yourself."**

Sabrina is an inspiration to young people because she is always true to herself. She is not afraid to be different, and she is an inspiration to young people who are struggling to find their own identity.

"Be yourself, and don't let anyone tell you who to be," Sabrina has said. **"You are amazing just the way you are."**

Sabrina is an inspiration to young people because she is a positive force in the world. She uses her platform to raise awareness about important social issues, and she is an inspiration to young people who want to make a difference.

Sabrina is an inspiration to young people in many ways. She is kind, caring, hardworking, talented, successful, and true to herself. She is an inspiration to young people who want to make a difference in the world.

"I'm so grateful for the opportunity to inspire others," Sabrina has said. **"It's the greatest honor of my life."**

Sabrina is an inspiration to millions of young people around the world. She is a positive force in the entertainment industry, and she uses her platform to inspire others to be their best selves. She is a great example of what it means to be a kind, caring, hardworking, talented, successful, and true to yourself. She is an inspiration to young people who want to make a difference in the world.

"**I believe that everyone has the power to make a difference,**" Sabrina has said. "**No matter how small, every act of kindness counts.**"

Sabrina is an inspiration to millions of young people around the world. She is a positive force in the entertainment industry, and she uses her platform to inspire others to be their best selves. She is a great example of what it means to be a kind, caring, hardworking, talented, successful, and true to yourself. She is an inspiration to young people who want to make a difference in the world.

A TIMELINE OF LIFE AND CAREER

- **1999**: Born in Philadelphia, Pennsylvania on May 11th.
- **Childhood**: Showed early interest in performing arts, often putting on shows for family and friends.
- **2011**: Landed her first acting role on the NBC drama series

"Law & Order: Special Victims Unit."

- **2012:** Cast as Riley Matthews in the Disney Channel series "Girl Meets World," a role that would bring her widespread recognition.

- **2014:** Signed a record deal with Hollywood Records and released her debut single, "Can't Blame a Girl for Trying."

- **2015**: Released her debut album, "Eyes Wide Open," featuring the hit singles "Why" and "Smoke and Fire."
- **2016**: Released her second album, "Evolution," and continued to tour extensively.
- **2017**: Starred in the Disney Channel movie "Adventures in Babysitting."
- **2018**: Released the album "Singular: Act I" and starred in

the film "The Short History of the Long Road."

- **2019:** Released "Singular: Act II" and starred in the film "Work It."
- **2020:** Made her Broadway debut in the musical "Mean Girls."
- **2021:** Signed with Island Records and released the single "Skin."

- **2022:** Released her fifth studio album, "emails i can't send," which was critically acclaimed.
- **2024:** Released her sixth studio album, "Short n' Sweet."

Sabrina Carpenter's career has been marked by her versatility as both a singer and actress. She continues to be a rising star in the entertainment industry.

GLOSSARY OF TERMS EXPLAINED

Album: A collection of songs recorded by a musician or band.

Audition: A trial performance to determine if someone is suitable for a role.

Charity: An organization that helps people in need.

Concert: A performance of music, often by a group of musicians.

Debut: The first appearance or release of something.

Genre: A category of artistic work, such as music or literature.

Hit: A song or album that is very popular.

Live Performance: A performance that is happening in real time, usually in front of an audience.

Lyrics: The words of a song.

Melody: A sequence of musical notes that form a tune.

Role Model: A person who serves as an example for others.

Tour: A series of performances in different locations.

Tune: A melody.

Versatility: The ability to do many different things well.

Voice Acting: The art of providing voices for animated characters or video games.

SABRINA CARPENTER QUIZ

Test your knowledge of Sabrina Carpenter!

1. What year was Sabrina Carpenter born?
   - A. 1990
   - B. 1995
   - C. 1999
   - D. 2004

2. In which Disney Channel show did Sabrina play the lead role?

    - A. Hannah Montana
    - B. Wizards of Waverly Place
    - C. Girl Meets World
    - D. Shake It Up

3. What is the name of Sabrina's first studio album?

    - A. Evolution
    - B. Singular
    - C. Emails I Can't Send

- D. Eyes Wide Open

4. What is the name of Sabrina's pet dog?

    - A. Max
    - B. Charlie
    - C. Buddy
    - D. Cooper

5. In which movie did Sabrina star alongside KJ Apa?

    - A. The Hate U Give
    - B. Looking Glass

- C. The Short History of the Long Road
- D. Work It

Answers:

1. **C.** 1999

2. **C.** Girl Meets World

3. **D.** Eyes Wide Open

4. **B.** Charlie

5. **A.** The Hate U Give

How did you do? Let me know your score in the comments!

Made in the USA
Monee, IL
01 May 2025

16722345R00085